STARTERS
SCIENCE

Rainbow
Colours

Macdonald Educational

The sun is shining through the rain drops.
We see a rainbow in the sky.
Sometimes the top is high.
Sometimes it is low.

2

Sometimes we can see two rainbows.
One is bright and the other is dim.
Have you ever tried to find
the end of a rainbow?

3

The water jets make a fine spray.
It is a sunny day.
Tiny drops of water split the sunlight
into colours.

4

Blow some bubbles.
Can you see the rainbow colours
on them?

Look at oil patches on wet roads.
Look through some glass shapes.
Look at the edges of mirrors.
Can you see the colours?

This glass tank is full of water.
Sunlight shines through the corner.
The light turns into rainbow colours.

These are the colours you can see
in a rainbow.
The names of rainbow colours are red,
orange, yellow, green, blue and purple.
8

matchstick stiff card

Make some spinning tops like these.
Spin them on a table or on the floor.
What happens to the colours?

Hold a small mirror in a dish of water.
Move the mirror a little.
Can you see colours on the ceiling
or on the wall?
10

Now stir up the water.
What happens to the colours?

11

Collect as many green things as you can.
Are all the greens the same?

12

Now collect as many red things as you can.
Try collecting other colours.
Are some colours harder to find
than others?

Flowers have many bright colours.
How many colours can you see here?

14

Many leaves change colour in autumn.
It is a good time to look for berries
and fruits.

Look at the dragonfly's wings.
Light shining on them
makes rainbow colours.

16

tiger moth

common blue butterfly

peacock butterfly

ladybirds

wasp

These insects have bright colours
and patterns on their bodies.

woodpecker

parakeet

blue tit

Many birds have beautiful coloured feathers.
Have you ever seen a blue tit?

18

There are brightly coloured things
all around us.
How many can you see here?

Can you see the bird in the tree?
Can you see the zebra and the tiger?
Patches and stripes help some animals
to hide.

20

Put a plain box in a leafy place.
Now paint the box to make it harder
to see.

These colours go well together.
Find some other colours
that go well together.

22

Red and green are very different colours.
We call them contrasting colours.
Can you think of some others?

These street lamps make a yellow light.
Some colours look different in yellow light.
Clothes and faces look strange.

shoe box

torch

tissue paper

Make a model stage.
Cover a torch with coloured tissue paper.
Shine different colours on the stage.
How does it look?

red plastic sheet

coloured glass

Find some coloured things to look through.
Does it make any difference
to the colours you see?

red cellophane

green cellophane

Make this colour signal.
Look at it through red cellophane.
Now look through green cellophane.
Are the colours the same each time?

Index